© 2023 By Stephen Daingerfield Dunn

All rights reserved.

This book, Or any portion thereof may not be reproduced or used in any manner whatsoever without express written permission of the author.

Printer in the united states of America

First edition, 2023

ISBN# 978-1088-279-93-9

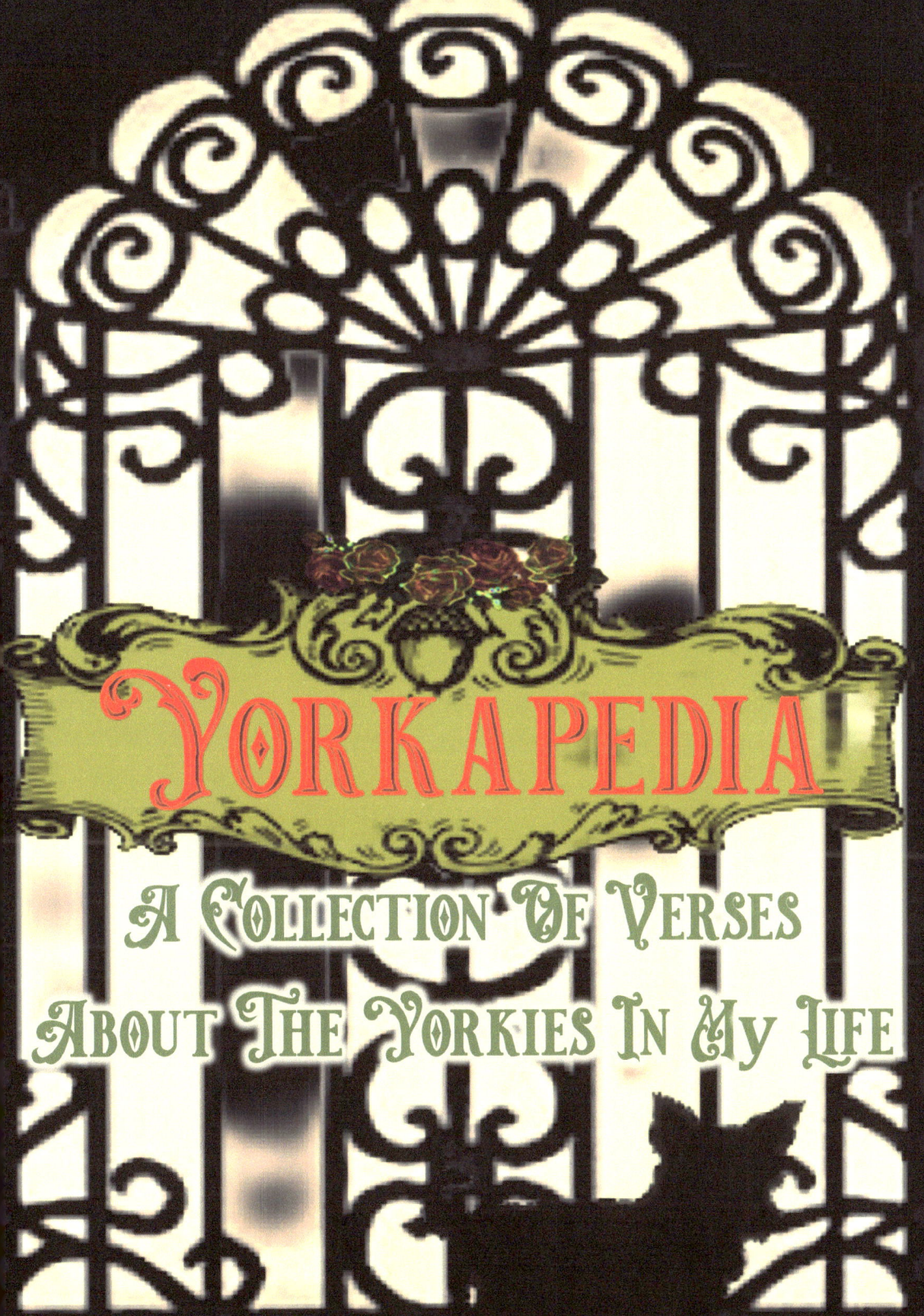

Table of Contents:

Introduction, Ultimate Love — Page 7

~Bianca~

God's Perfect Creatures — Page 11
My Girl And Me — Page 15
Heart Breaker — Page 19
Perfect Pet Love — Page 21

~Zoe~

Our Special Girl — Page 25
Raw Pain — Page 29
Perfect Memory Moments — Page 33
Devoted Companion — Page 35
Perfect Pups — Page 39

~Camilla~

Precious Pup — Page 43
Camilla Forever — Page 47
Happy Birthday Camilla — Page 49
On Being Camilla — Page 53

~Fifi~

Another Fifi Tail Wagger — Page 57
Fifi Fiona — Page 61
Forever Fifi — Page 65
Have I Told You About Fifi? — Page 67
Most Beautiful Girl In The World — Page 71

~Tallulah~

And Tallulah Makes Five — Page 75
Fur And Fun — Page 77
Yet Another Precious Gift — Page 81

Ultimate Love – An Introduction

It seems more often than not
I look forward to those evenings with you,
Just us and our 2 puppies
Where we have very little else to do.

We cuddle with one another,
As we tousle our furry friends,
Holding on to each other,
Believing that the future will never end.

Its so simple to love them,
For they are innocent and easy to embrace,
Even when they get rambunctious,
And want to give you kisses upon the face.

We hear the clock ticking,
As we wile away the hours,
Knowing that every minute is valuable,
And each one should be thoroughly devoured.

No matter the number of rhymes,
That I feel are dedicated to our pups,
I can never exaggerate enough,
What their aura has brought to us.

Nothing like that kind of pure love,
As you look into their eyes,
Because no matter how clever they may be,
That is one thing they cannot disguise.

No matter how endearing my words may be,
I can never say how deeply I feel,
But hopefully when you read this rhyme,
You will know that they are sincere and real.

God's Perfect Creatures

They rule our lives
for a few short years,
bringing us laughter
and happiness tears.

Stealing our hearts and souls
with their perfect love,
obviously sent here
from heaven up above.

Shaggy and short
sleek and tall,
something to adore
about them all.

We try to train them
to do their best,
but I have to say
that can be a lifelong test.

So much innocence
in God's perfect creatures,
they rule our homes
and become our best teachers.

Just a gentle pat
or maybe a tummy scratch,
that's all they wish for
as they lay on their backs.

Never are the days long enough
that they live in our homes,
waiting there patiently
for their next bone.

So, on this beautiful day
we bless their little souls,
knowing they are our prizes
worth more than a pot of gold.

No matter their shape or color
no matter their breed or size,
they will always be God's perfect creatures
at least in our loving eyes.

Nothing in this whole world
can take the place of our pets,
the most perfect companions
that I've ever met.

Happy to see me
even when I scold,
I shall hold them in reverence
as we both grow old.

I thank you once again
my dear amazing God,
for what would life be like
without my precious cat or dog.

My Girl and Me

Snuggled up,
My girl and me,
Every night,
Her place to be.

Feeling her by me
Touching my side,
My girl and me
Along for the ride.

Loving devotion,
We cuddle and coo,
A love for each other,
Every night we renew.

A beauty so fair,
With her delicate features,
A perfect example
Of God's perfect creatures.

Returning each evening
to nestle with me,
no place on earth
she would rather be.

Delicate curls
and big black eyes,
that we love one another
comes as no surprise.

Who in the world
would I rather see
than my little girl,
huddled close to me.

An angel on earth,
she sleeps by my side,
happy to snuggle
my joyful pride.

A tiny miracle
this girl of mine,
never a question
where her love resides.

Three pounds of joy
my furry bronze pup,
we would just as soon sleep
and never get up.

My petite girl named Bianca,
my girlfriend in bed,
always beside me,
with very little to be said.

I love her dearly
and she loves me too,
my girl and me
forever true...

Heart Breaker

I look down into those tiny black eyes
that appear to be filled with love,
that kind of devotion and adoration
we have for only God up above.

Bianca Bronte

What is she sincerely thinking
in her tiny little canine mind?
I want to believe if she could speak
it would make my life truly shine.

Daily she becomes more precious
with her habits and loving licks,
because trust me if you pucker up
she's gonna give you a big old wet kiss.

3 or maybe 4 pounds
of fur, teeth and bones,
nobody in the whole world could be happier to see you
when you finally get back home.

She brings you her favorite raggedy toy
the one she has had since birth,
the one that will always be her favorite
though it's covered with food and dirt.

It appears that she has a sly little smile
when she travels up the bed to find your face,
especially at 4:30 a.m. in the morning
long before you've even joined the human race.

Forever and always a puppy
and we pray that she never grows old,
in fact I lecture her each and every morning
and tell her she has at least 15 more years to go!

Perfect Pet Love

Precious creatures
God's perfect gift.
They give our souls
a heavenly lift.

Nothing can match
the love of a pet,
given purely
with no regrets.

Trusting us implicitly
to be their friend,
faithful and loyal
to the very end.

Perfect innocence
emits from their eyes,
a true loyalty
that they cannot disguise.

They anxiously await
for us to come home,
ever so happy
when you toss them that bone.

Racing madly
from space to space,
ever so excited to see
that smile upon your face.

Never has there been
a purer devotion,
than these caring canines
with their heartfelt emotions.

They are our children
for a period of time,
far too short
a heartbreaking crime.

We know the minute
they enter our lives,
the time will be short
we can treasure those eyes.

So, embrace their spirit
for it belonged to you,
just ever so happy
though their years were few.

Nothing in the world
can ever replace,
that look of pure joy
they wore on their face.

So, treasure the memories
and lay them to rest,
the years we loved them
were the very best.

Our Special Girl ~ Zoe Theodora Moet
(2001 - November 23rd, 2012)

She came into this life,
her challenges were not few,
it was suggested by some
she might not make it through.

Like a tiny furry caterpillar
that fit into a coffee cup,
we lovingly watched her
as she awkwardly grew up.

Happy in her home
consuming her much-loved food,
she toddled when she walked
always in a good mood.

She shook when it thundered
as the rainstorms poured,
She paced our bedroom for miles
and steadily walked the floor.

One could only surmise
as she lay at our feet,
Sleeping beneath our bed
she hardly made a peep.

Rarely her wish
 to ever be touched,
But wanting our special love
when it showed up.

With a face like an angel
and heart much the same,
She never had a chance
in life's little game.

Now on her birthday
eleven years have gone,
she has given this life up
which somehow seems wrong.

Our sadness is immeasurable
as tears leave their trace,
I write her last story
and think of that dear face.

I cannot believe she's gone
as I see her breathlessly racing,
running beneath my clothes
with some ghost she's chasing.

Being precious Zoe
in her own special world,
being her own creation
my crazy little girl...

Raw Pain, Pure Love and Sad Feelings - A Tribute To Zoe

Raw
Burning
Unshakeable
Pain.

Open wound
gaping sore
hardly breathing
barely sane.

Hurt beyond
my deepest measure.
No consolation
no sign of pleasure.

Zoe Theodora Moet

Yet bound in this knot
of endless despondence,
is this essence of love
a very odd cadence.

A love of such pureness
it frightens the soul.
A love of such sweetness
not many will hold.

I wish you back
to finish this dance.
I wish your return
and one more chance.

To hold you close
to kiss your sweet face.
To hold you close
in this sacred space.

But sadness has bloomed
and spread its quiet pain.
For you have silently departed
while I still remain.

No return to be expected
My eyes shed soft tears.
They creep down my face
as I yearn for you to be here.

Just to adore your sweet gentle grace
and to tell you how much I care,
just to live one more precious moment
to be without this sadness and despair…

Perfect Memory Moments

Peace and solitude surround me
as I sit in the warmth of my car,
accompanied by my two perfect puppies
who are my best friends by far.

The radio is playing softly
a song which brings up memories from the past,
a tune that reminds me of my sister
and the day that she passed.

As salty tears cloud my vision
a pure white heron soars up to the sky,
as I remanence about Sarah Brightman singing
that it is time to say goodbye.

I feel the warmth of the winter sun
as it shines upon my face,
and this is now a memory in my life
that shall never be erased.

One of my canine babies
is sound asleep in her tiny bed,
and her breathing makes a soft little sound
that rambles around in my head.

The trees are barren and beautiful
and I hear the creek trickling nearby,
and I reluctantly head back to our home
with a smile and a sweet long sigh.

Devoted Companions

Profound devotion,
no questions asked,
like loving companions,
from out of the past.

Large black eyes
that pierce the soul,
seemingly wise
no matter how old.

Happy to see us
or so it would seem,
panting profusely
they lovingly beam.

Running for hours
a racing machine,
frolicking forever
no sin to redeem.

Never to suffer
 a day of bad moods,
simply happy
to have more food!

Quietly obedient
standing at your feet,
wagging their tails
for their favorite treat.

Sad when you leave them,
excited at your return,
never one small doubt,
never to be concerned.

How can they know
when our world turns upside down,
how can they perceive
it's them we need around.

Never would a human
love with so much trust,
never can we match
the love of one small mutt.

Perhaps they are angels
dressed in furry suits,
I know they make me happy
when it's love I pursue

Perfect Pups

Our pups are precious,
petite indeed,
They bring us great pleasure
with very few needs.

They scamper and play
living life day by day,
and we surely wouldn't have it
any other way.

How could so much love
be in a gift so small?
Guarding our home diligently,
no intruder too tall.

Licks of adoration
or was it from our last snack?
Whatever the reason
we welcome those tongue attacks.

They snuggle with one another,
a miracle we are told,
two girls in one house
a sight to behold.

They look into our eyes
with full faith and trust,
knowing we will care for them
as we well know we must.

God's little creatures
bless us every day,
doing it without restrictions
in their own perfect way.

Loyal and devoted
it works both ways,
they will always be the best children
in each and every way.

Fi Fi and Camilla
the winners of the prize,
being absolutely perfect
no matter their size.

We thank you dear Lord
no matter the years,
just blessed to enjoy them
these two precious dears…

Precious Pup

A tiny little puppy,
left sad and alone,
only an appliance box
to be her day long home.

Camilla Simone

Never allowed
to make a squeak,
much less bark
or havoc would wreak.

Taking her soul
and dimming her light,
no longer allowed
to put up a fight.

Quietly she survived
without a sound,
that extra sense
that she could be put down.

Finally, when the wardens
were destined to leave town,
it was sell her for cash
or, put her in the pound.

Then the miracle happened
and her savior appeared,
no intention of saving
this precious little dear.

But save her he did
with valor and pride,
took her away
to a life by his side.

Still to this day,
her sweet little soul,
reminds us of one
who is very, very old.

Her moments of joy
are few and far between,
but we know that she feels
all the love that she's seen.

A sweeter pup
you will never find,
gentle and devout,
a one-of-a-kind.

Christened with a new name,
as well as a home,
there's not a dearer girl
than our Camilla Simone!

Camilla Forever

I lay here in my bed
staring at you eye-to-eye,
our darling silver princess
who deserves a grand prize.

She is regal and composed
in her very own Camilla way,
and we treasure and adore her
every moment of every single day.

Her coat is platinum and glossy
just like a canine super star,
and she has shown us her brilliance
that can be seen near and far.

We treasure each year and minute
that God has kept her alive,
as I gratefully feel blessed every morning
when she opens those big black eyes.

We doubt that she truly hears much
and not sure of what she sees,
but she can still be vivacious and frolic
and can bring us to our knees.

An angel brought to earth
though we had to rescue her from hell,
however, if she could tell you of her life with us
I think she would say it's been quite a magical fairy tale...

Happy Birthday Camilla

A brave little princess
our Camilla Simone,
starting off her life
sequestered and alone.

Kept in a cardboard box
eight hours a day,
never given the opportunity
to bark and play.

Deserted for hours
with no place to roam,
her only tiny concept
of what must be home.

But rescue her we did
and brought her to our world,
knowing that she knew
she was one lucky little girl.

She could easily win her category
in the A.K.A.,
the most beautiful of her breed
we simply have to say.

With her silver platinum coat
and black diamond eyes,
she would most surely capture
most any canine prize.

A more loving puppy
you will never hope to see,
as long as you give her time
and just let her be.

Calm and serene
she rules our little domain,
with very few barks
nor reasons to complain.

Curled up sweetly
upon her favorite bed,
a specimen of the very finest
Yorkie ever bred.

So, on her Birthday
we wish her the very best,
eleven years of life
and some pretty tough tests.

But that is in her past
and she resides with us now,
a treasure we shall cherish
for it is our eternal vow.

Beautiful Camilla
a treasure that is ours,
happy at last
as she frolics for hours.

On Being Camilla

I wonder what you're thinking
My darling distant child
With your sweet disposition
And what appears to be a smile

Looking at me squarely
Right between the eyes
With what looks to be sadness
But still so very wise

I feel that her trust
Is still somewhat shy
By that sad bit of fear
That she cannot disguise

Nothing seems to faze her
This sweet little pup
Though we do not wish to linger
On what she went through growing up

A prize of such beauty
With her silver platinum fur
To imagine her mistreated
Is a thought I do not prefer

Sitting by the fireplace
Eyes riveted on me
Secure at last
For the whole world to see

And still the sadness
That fills her eyes
Makes me angry
With the desire to cry

A cruel beginning
That marked her life
Even though now
She suffers no strife

I chose to believe
That deep in her soul
She is eternally grateful
If the truth be told

A wee tiny princess
With those dark amber eyes
Perhaps just another angel
In a doggie disguise

Precious sweet Camilla
Rescued at last
Living in her dream
Never looking back

Another Fifi Tail Wagger

Fifi Fiona

A three-pound pup
just fur and bone,
rules the roost
and runs our home.

A happier dog
I shall never see,
nothing more amazing
than our baby Fifi.

She greets us daily
no matter the time,
jumping with excitement
being one-of-a-kind.

Running in circles
just happy to be,
a dog without boundaries
as you will soon see.

Dare to take her
close to your face,
her tongue can be the fastest
in any kissing race.

Devouring her chew sticks
ten at a time,
dragging her toys
from your lap to mine.

Sparkling black eyes
like two tiny bits of coal,
ears that are at attention
never doing as she is told.

Sleeping with contentment
after a hard day of fun,
she knows in her little brain
our hearts have been won.

Back up at dawn
with youth on her side,
she runs to the door
to monitor outside.

Barking at a worm
a leaf or a bird,
perhaps it was another dog
she thinks she has heard.

Keeping all predators
safely at bay,
doing it with authority
in her very frightening way.

Never will there ever
be another like her,
three pounds of energy
with white teeth and black fur.

Fififiona

Every day
is a special day!
Nothing at all
can stand in her way!

Endless energy
plenty to spare,
racing around madly
her joy to share.

Always ecstatic
this 3 pounds of joy,
a gift from above
a wind-up toy!

A package of pleasure
utter delight,
never stopping for a moment
until day becomes night.

How does she manage
to make the world spin,
an attitude to copy
a case of win-win.

Fi Fi Fiona,
a puppy with speed.
Just give her a minute
that's all she needs!

Fastest tongue
 in the whole wide West,
whole face licks
the very, very best!

Many a pup
we've been blessed to own,
but never one like this
has lived in our home!

God give me the gift
to learn from her zeal,
life can be joyful
when you can just be real.

So, treasure the minutes
we share with this pup,
because trust me my dear
she will never give up!

Forever Fifi

She most definitely possesses
a mind of her own.
One of the smartest pups
that we've ever owned.

One of her Dads calls her "Biscuit,"
while the other Dad calls her "Frog",
however, her real name is "Fifi"
and she is one-hell-of-a-dog!

Three and a half pounds of Yorkie
That possesses energy and feist,
Always willing to be challenged
to jump to any height.

She tolerates our love and affection
as we spoil her every day,
but trust me in the end
she will always have it her way.

Racing up and down steep stairs
like no pup has ever done before,
striking a pose that steals our heart
who could ask for anything more.

She has her little fears
like when the thunder claps,
and occasionally a little nightmare
when she decides to take a nap.

Taking over our bed
sleeping wherever she desires,
giving me ideas for my poems
which she has obviously inspired.

Fifi Fiona,
with those tiny black eyes that touch our heart,
giving us those kisses every morning
that give our day a perfect start!

Have I Told You About Fifi?

Four pounds of fur and love
that illuminates our lives,
helping us survive this unusual year
of fear, depression and plight.

She adores us faithfully
and welcomes us each time we come home,
perhaps it's all in the fact
that she wants a brand-new bone!

However, it matters not
for she is cheerful most every day,
and God knows the rest of the world
doesn't seem to see things that way.

She cuddles by our sides
and snuggles when she's in the mood,
but unlike human beings
she is never distant or rude.

So much love and innocence
Wrapped up in one little pup.
She magically transforms our world
From the minute we arise and get up.

In these times of a world of depressed people
She brings us sweet relief,
For her little innocent mind
Knows nothing about viruses and grief.

A precious little life saver
We are fortunate enough to own,
For she certainly brings her warmth and adoration
To this place we call home.

A slight little bit of a dog
With a personality bigger than life,
That treasure we call Fifi Fiona
Who is always a daily delight!

So, thank you dearest God,

For all of the critters we have been blessed to treasure.

But, thank you especially for this tiny little gift that has brought us so much company and pleasure!

Most Beautiful Girl in The World

If love is the elixir
that makes one truly fly,
then it will be your destiny
to soar through the sky.

To float with the angels
because you're adored near and far,
always and forever
that bright shining star.

Though it seems to be impossible
that you could be worshipped anymore,
there simply is no known way
that one could possibly keep score.

However, the very dearest part
is the love that you give in return,
that day after day feeling
that makes my heart burn.

Looking ever so deeply
into those amber black eyes,
makes me so very happy
I almost wish to cry.

I pray that your precious lifespan
will easily match that of mine,
just being by my side
for the remainder of all time.

Though you're petite and small in statue
there is still plenty to worship and adore,
even the way you sprint
makes me love you even more and more.

How can all of that magic
be contained within such a tiny soul,
it makes me want to take you
everywhere that I go.

So, my forever precious Fifi,
who brings us so much laughter and fun,
you will always be the best 4-pound prize
that we were blessed to have ever won.

And Tallulah Makes Five

Showing up like magic,
coming from out of thin air,
this tiny bit of canine
which is now in our loving care.

Tallulah Tulip

How can a pound of bone and fur
suddenly disrupt our house and home?
It feels like she dropped down from heaven
no matter that she arrived here all alone.

A creature like none other
that we have been blessed to receive,
such an adorable treasure
that it seems totally impossible to believe.

However here she is,
one tiny ball of delight.
Even though she has made it almost impossible
to sleep through one whole night.

We want to hold her constantly,
tight to our beating heart,
and yet somehow we must teach her
what it is like to be apart.

Surely, we will be guided
to keep her safe in every way,
for we have learned more and more about her
during every single hour of the day.

We must be extra careful
to pay attention to the reigning queen,
for as far as our precious girl named Fifi goes
nobody can ever come in between.

And yet we know she will grow quickly
and we must cherish her while we can,
for their love and intense loyalty
is far deeper than any woman or man.

Welcome home sweet Tallulah

you have instantly stolen our hearts.

Who knew the sadness it would bring

the first occasion that we were apart...

Fur And Fun

Four pounds of shiny fur
filled with love and fun.
She will be the one who saves me
when this is all over and done.

She could care less
about the news of the day.
And God only knows what I would give
to live my life the very same way.

She always greets me
with that little pink tongue,
treating me as always
like I'm the only one.

With those tiny sparkling black eyes,
as well as that precious smile,
these are what I shall treasure always
as though she were my only child.

Bouncing about gaily
on her dainty little paws,
You would think she was a kid
and I was Santa Claus.

Few are the beings in life
who are in a good mood every day,
but she is always there to greet me
in her very own special little way.

As we snuggle into bed for the evening
she delivers one last kiss,
a very special moment
that I never try to miss.

One little furry angel
that shall always own my heart and soul,
planning to share life together
until we both grow very, very old.

Yet Another Precious Gift

And as these Yorkie stories continue,
Along came our latest prize.
A little bit of a demon
Because you can see it in her eyes.

Barely 2 months old,
She has very little fear,
Settling in immediately
Like she had always been here.

Terrorizing her older sister,
Who has no room for this little mutt,
As we stand by and make a wish
That she will quickly grow-up.

And as the saga goes along,
With each new princess that we possess,
This one for sure has her own personality,
And from there I shall digress.

A PETITE 2 POUNDS OF BEAUTY,
WITH A BARK THAT PIERCES THE EAR.
SHE CERTAINLY DOES NOT HESITATE
TO LET YOU KNOW SHE IS HERE.

WHEN SHE STRETCHES HER TINY TORSO,
OUT ON TO THE GREEN LAWN,
WE KNOW OUR LOVE HAS BEEN CAPTURED
AN THAT WE COULD STAY THERE UNTIL DAWN.

HOW CAN THIS TINY PARCEL
JUST TROT IN AND WIN OUR HEARTS?
I CANNOT TELL YOU THE ANSWER
BUT IT WAS THAT WAY FROM THE VERY START.

I SHALL END MY ONGOING PUPPY TALES
BUT YOU CAN BE SURE THERE WILL BE MORE.
SO BE SURE TO LOOK FOR MY NEXT BOOK
ABOUT THIS PUPPY THAT WE FIND HARD TO IGNORE.

www.ingramcontent.com/pod-product-compliance
Lightning Source LLC
Chambersburg PA
CBHW041433010526
44118CB00002B/59